How to Draw

CARTOON® NETWORK

Scooby-Doo!™

Written by Jesse Leon McCann
Illustrated by Eddie Young

WB WORLDWIDE PUBLISHING™

Walter Foster™

TOOLS OF THE TRADE

Hi, kids! As Scooby and the gang solve another exciting mystery, you'll learn how to draw our intrepid heroes and other cool things!

Just as a detective needs clues, an artist needs tools. You'll need some grid paper, a pencil, a black felt-tip pen, a variety of colored felt-tip markers—get fat and skinny points—and maybe some colored pencils. Keep a pencil sharpener and eraser handy too.

CARNIVAL CLOSED

Grid paper makes it easy to draw our super sleuths in action. You can buy grid paper, or you can make your own—which is a lot more fun! Use a ruler to make evenly spaced, straight lines for the grid—1/2- to 1-inch squares are best. After you make your grid, you might want to make photocopies of it so you can draw all day long!

tting Started

'll also need to know a few tricks of the trade. Drawings
basically a bunch of different lines and shapes. Start by
king a lot of curved lines and circles. Be sure to keep your
n loose and relaxed. Draw with your whole arm, not just
ur wrist.

All warmed up and ready to get
tarted? Now just follow the easy
step-by-step drawings in this
ook, copying the blue lines you
see in each step onto your grid
paper. Notice where the lines
should touch the grid. Try to make
your drawing match the example.
hat's all there is to it!

"There's Mr. Withers, the carnival
manager," explains Velma. "Maybe
he can tell us why all the local
people say the carnival is haunted!"

"Gulp! Raunted?"
Scooby asks nervously.

THE MYSTERY MACHINE

1 HEAD

Keeping It in Proportion

Speaking of proportion, here's a height chart to help you keep the characters' proportions in order as you draw them. Artists use the head as a unit of measurement. Each lined section on this chart represents 1 head length, so Shaggy and Freddy are 7 heads tall, and Velma is almost 6 heads tall.

Scooby has a big head! Give him a large muzzle and a long, thick neck.

Draw a wide grin and bright eyes. Then fill in his big nose and bushy brows.

Scooby—Ahead of It All
Because Scooby is hiding behind the headstones, this is a good opportunity to learn how to draw his head. Do it quick—he's about to get nabbed!

As the gang investigates the gloomy mansion, they stumble upon the library.

Shaggy—Heads Up

Shaggy will be okay! After all, he's got a pretty good head on his shoulders. While we're on the subject, here's how to draw Shaggy's head.

Shaggy has a long, narrow face, a thick mop of hair, and a pencil-thin neck.

Give him a big smile—as if he just spotted a pepperoni pizza.

Shaggy rarely combs his hair—and he always has a few whiskers on his chin.

Now color in his mop top.

"This book tells of a vast pirate treasure, still hidden somewhere near where the carnival stands today," Freddy explains.

"And this journal has a clue to where the treasure is buried," Velma adds excitedly. "'I have one eye, yet nothing escapes my sight—I'm tall and strong, but also light.' Whatever could it mean?"

Suddenly, a secret passage opens in one of the bookshelves. Zoinks!

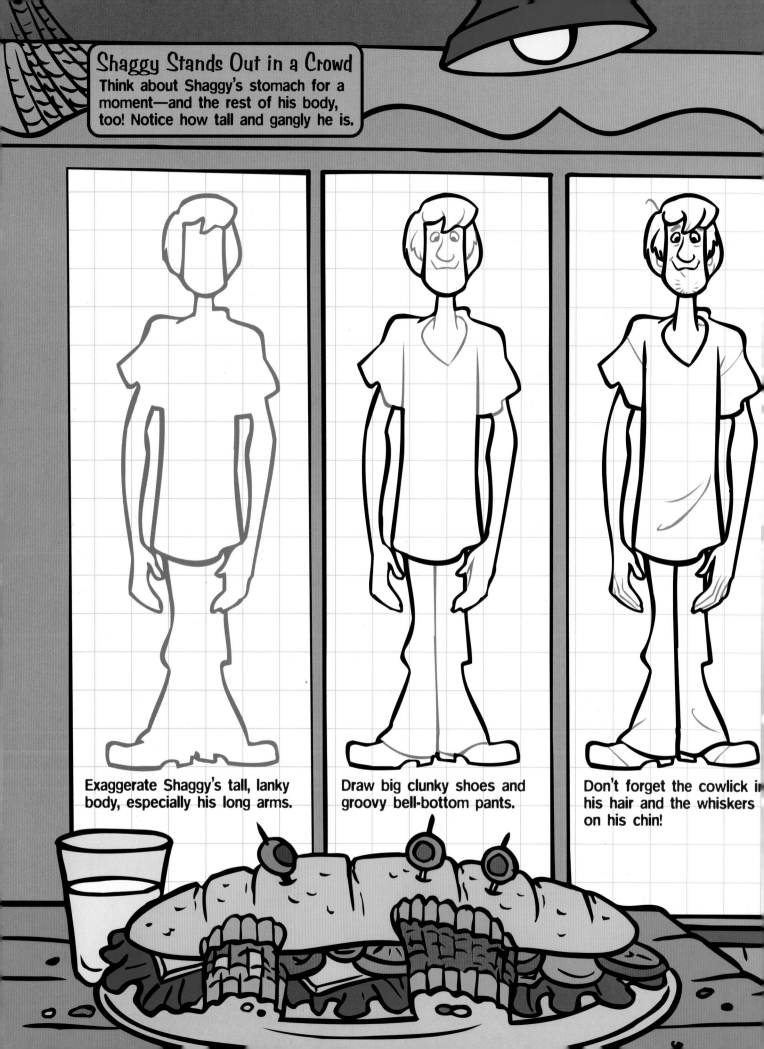

Shaggy Stands Out in a Crowd

Think about Shaggy's stomach for a moment—and the rest of his body, too! Notice how tall and gangly he is.

Exaggerate Shaggy's tall, lanky body, especially his long arms.

Draw big clunky shoes and groovy bell-bottom pants.

Don't forget the cowlick in his hair and the whiskers on his chin!

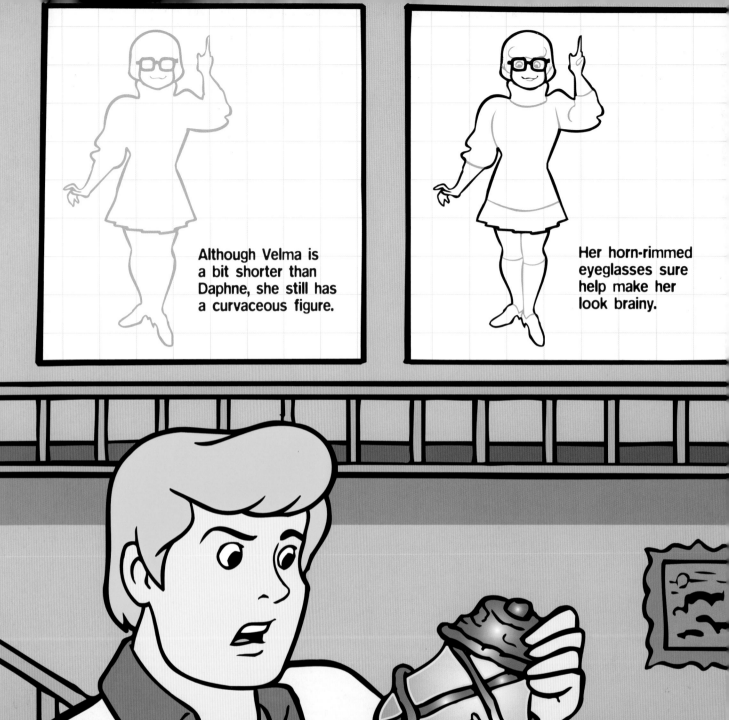

Although Velma is a bit shorter than Daphne, she still has a curvaceous figure.

Her horn-rimmed eyeglasses sure help make her look brainy.

Really exaggerate the enormous, hunched shoulders and blocky form.

Notice how low the head sits on this oversized, no-necked monster.

DOING THE MONSTER MASH
Zoinks! It looks as if there are two monsters in the house! This one is a lot bigger than the mummy, and his body is lopsided and freakish. Keep this in mind as you draw him.

Fleeing the creature, Scooby and Shaggy hide in a dark room. They soon realize they're not alone.

"A good thing you opened that door," Freddy says. "Those fiends locked us in!"

This one isn't as hard as it looks—really! Just take your time, and follow the steps.

Don't forget those proportions! The height chart on page 4 will help you here.

HAIL—The Gang's All Here!
Hooray! The gang is back together and fresh on the scent! Now's a good time to draw a group shot.

Now just add the details. Try to capture each character's expression.

Color their outfits as shown—or give them a new wardrobe. It's up to you!

"Like, it looks like they left this so you could dig your way out, ya dig?" Shaggy remarks, holding up a shovel with fresh dirt on it.

"Jinkies! What on earth would two creatures like that be doing with a shovel?" asks Velma, thoughtfully.

There's No Place Like Home

Before the gang leaves, take a look at how to create a haunted mansion on paper.

Don't make your lines *too* perfect—keep 'em spooky!

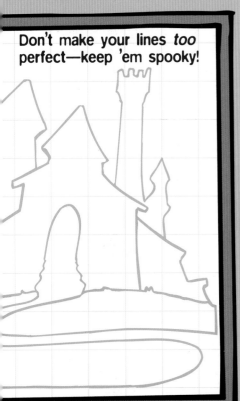

Distort the shapes of the windows to make them look eerie.

dd some dead shrubbery and few bats around the "belfry."

Then color.

"Bwah-ha-ha-ha!" laughs the evil clown, greeting them at the carnival entrance.

"Run, Scoob!" yells Shaggy.

Here is the corrupt clown, poised to attack.

Give the face a sinister grin and masklike eyes.

Just Clowning Around

Clowns are supposed to be fun. But as you draw this one, you can see that he's not!

The big, baggy costume needs only a few final touches.

Now add some color to bring this villain to life.

Then color it in.

Add the wispy clouds for interest.

"The lantern Freddy found is the kind lighthouse keepers have," Daphne realizes, "and I'll bet that shovel was used to dig up the treasure!"

"Treasure like that gold coin Scooby found!" Shaggy adds, "and now they're trying to load the loot onto that boat."

"Shhh!" whispers Freddy. "If we're quiet, we can sneak up and nab them in the act."

The Light at the End of the Tunnel

od for Velma! A lighthouse is! Did you figure it out ? Here you see how to aw that lighthouse yourself.